Houseless people in the United States are intended to be silenced, to be surrounded by useless platitudes and cliches. The disease of forced silence can only be healed by cherishing the words of those whom no one was intended to listen to. Within this cover are the lost words that are now found. Cherish.
-Pastor Steven Kimes, Eugene, Oregon

This is beautiful and amazing and so moving. I heartily endorse!!!
-Laura Golino de Lovato, Executive Director NW Pilot Project

Like hundreds of secrets being whispered into my heart from voices dreaming to be heard. Voices with spirit, and God, in the wild, and full of resistance. Beautiful, determined, lovely resistance is weaved deeply within the stories and visions of every poem.

-Kristle Delihanty, Founder/Executive Director PDX Saints Love

We often hear about giving the marginalised a voice. When so often what they need is for us to give them our ears. This great little book gives you an opportunity to do so. Get reading and listening.

-Eagle Spits punk poet and founder of Punk 4 The Homeless

Flowers of the Litter speaks from and to the human spirit – indomitable, always hopeful, and smouldering with the embers of aliveness in spite of formidable odds…The homeless may not have a place to shelter in but their minds are home to thoughts, emotions, longings, and the need to connect with others at some level; they are as strong, as weak as the rest of the 'privileged' beings who inhabit this globe. This collection of poems seeks to address their concerns; describe their condition, while recognizing their fundamental dignity as human beings. The poems are poignant - and uplifting – and linger on in the imagination.

-Malati Mathur, Creative Writer and Translator and Fellow at the Indian Institute of Advanced Study, Shimla. Professor of English; former Director, School of Humanities and School of Foreign Languages, IGNOU, N Delhi

Endorsements for Flowers of the Litter

"The poems that comprise *Flowers of the Litter* are compelling because they express the raw emotion and trauma of being houseless. But this is not to say the poetry is sad because they filled me with joy and wonder. The words "hope" and "love" occur over and over in the poems, and the poets speak of friendship, community, gratitude, and laughter. The poets speak of grace, kindness, and charity, but not that they receive from nonprofits but of the grace, kindness, and charity they give to one another. *Flowers of the Litter* provides a window in the community and family that exists among our unsheltered neighbors. In "Haiku" by Resa Alboher, the speaker proclaims, "We want to fly too." In this profound collection of poems, these poets not only fly but soar."
-Scott Kerman, Executive Director of Blanchet House, Portland

The collection of poetry contained in this book allows us to see each other, hear each other, and remember we are all connected. We are all in this together.
-Sisters of the Road, Portland

FLOWERS OF THE LITTER is not just another collection of poems. This is an outstanding anthology of subtle and gentle activist poems, that centre the misery of the hapless, homeless folks, who live under the skies, moving from street to street, living on scraps of leftovers like hungry scavengers. The timeless voice of Walt Whitman resonates in the excerpts juxtaposed alongside the voices of 21st century living poets, reminding readers that our much canvassed progress has been selective and discriminatory, the irony of cyclical progression, trapped between change and continuity. The anguish and protest in these poems do not incite anger. Instead, as the poet and editor Mimi German states in her preamble, the poems included in FLOWERS OF THE LITTER spur a wakeup call by striving to ignite our sense of empathy for those who we see and hear and yet see and hear them not.

-Dr. Sanjukta Dasgupta, President, Executive Committee, Intercultural Poetry and Performance Library, Kolkata, Visiting Professor, Jagiellonian University, Krakow, Poland (2018)
Honorary Visiting Professor, Dept. of English, Sister Nivedita University

"This collection of poems is how those that struggle mark the seconds of their day, not in plans for the future but worries for the present, examining what it means to be desperate with hope for change. Time marked only by the existence of the sun."

-Z D Dicks is Gloucestershire Poet Laureate (UK) and has read his work on BBC radio, his poems have been used as interactive features for the 'Poetry in the Priories' project

Flowers
Of the litter

Poetry of and for People
Living on the Streets

Selected by

Mimi German & Karlostheunhappy

EYEPUBLISHEWE

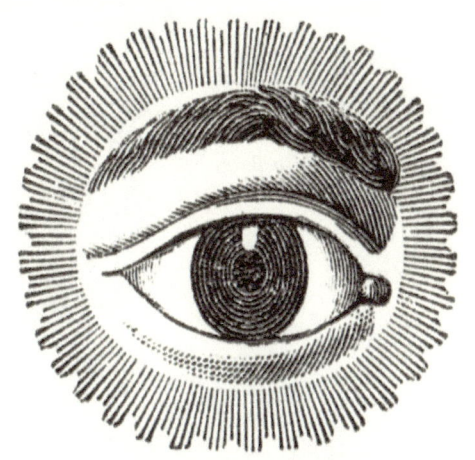

PUBLISH

PUBLISHING POETRY, LITERATURE, ART, MUSIC
FOR HUMANITY'S SAKE
A BRANDNEW PUBLISHING COMPANY
SAN FRANCISCO
FOUNDED 2020

and a voice in court yells…

"I don't believe the voices of skid row have been heard"

'General' Jeff Page
(1965 - 2021)

Mayor of Skid Row

Acknowledgements

This collection has been curated by Mimi German, with assistance from Karlostheunhappy.

Mimi would like to express her thanks and acknowledgement first and foremost to Street Roots for all of their support on this project and, of course, thanks also to the *Street Roots* poets.

Frontispiece quote from the LA Times 'The powerful legacy of General Jeff Page, West Coast hip-hop pioneer and 'mayor of skid row' by G. Holland, 2nd November 2021.

(https://www.latimes.com/california/story/2021-11-02/general-jeff-mayor-of-skid-row-and-west-coast-hip-hop-pioneer-dies?)

Mimi would like also to thank Oregon Poet Laureate, Kim Stafford, for suggesting the idea of this little book.

Our deepest thanks to the following authors for allowing us to use their work in this anthology...

Smokestack Books for allowing us to include Fred Voss' fine poem, 'No One Works as Hard as the Homeless' which originally appeared in *Someday There Will Be Machine Shops Full of Roses* (F. Voss, Smokestack Books, 2023).

'It Hurts So Good To Be Alive' by Bill Lewis, which originally appeared in his collection *This Love Like A Rage Without Anger: poems 1975-2005* (**Colony Press**, 2019)

George Wallace appears courtesy of **Roadside Press**. His contribution was written especially for this collection.

Karlostheunhappy appears courtesy of **Gloomy for Pleasure** (GloomyForPleasure.com). 'Stoned' and 'Minimalist Poem' by Karlostheunhappy written especially for this anthology but also appears in the author's second collection also due in 2024, *FLUX: the turning leaves* (Gloomy for Pleasure).

Foreword: 'To My Houseless Friends'

by "Preacher Steve" Kimes

May no one steal your anger, not even yourself. Keep it as a pilot light, allowing your fury to feed the compassion and the actions of others.

May you not be overcome by anger so that you are not feared to be threatening.

May you be strong when interacting with the housed.

Did that person mean to insult you or tear you down? Most likely. As a people, we have yet to learn how to care for and respect others as we wish to be respected.

May the dehumanizers never place their cancer in your heart or breath.

May you only give a permanent place in your thoughts to those who grant you a place to be fully yourself.

May you never cease to long for and pursue a better life, even if you must leave some friends behind.

Humanity is better served by having one person pulled out of a drowning sea than to have ten drown because they didn't accept the hand that could pull them out of the water. Take as many people out as you can when you leave the place of despair. However, if you are the only one who can escape, do it.

May you never trust or believe in authorities. They are only interested in maintaining and growing their power, and you don't have any strength they are interested in. Ignore them, avoid them, if you can.

May you never be silent to those who dehumanize you. If someone blocks your path of survival, make sure they know exactly what they are doing to a fellow human being, a fellow citizen, a fellow neighbor whom they should love. On the final day, may they have no excuse to have stripped you of days or weeks of living.

May you never be silent. May you scream when you need to scream; may you shout at your demons. It is more healthy to rage at them than give in to them.

May we need to vent our fury at the world that has taken everything from us. Sometimes we just need to explode at a stranger to speak of how we have been treated unfairly. In this, may we still remember how we are seen by a stranger. How we are seen as 'crazy' even when we are not. We are seen as 'irrational' even when we are more logical in this insane world than they. We are seen as dangerous, when they are the ones who have killed us, every day, slowly, one phone call at a time.

If possible, may we never rage at those who have been there for us.

May we not damage the wall that supports us, even if it is broken and sometimes does a terrible job of holding us up.

May you have the opportunity to explain quietly, to be heard about your sorrows and the difficulties in your life.

May someone grant you all your heart needs to be reassured. You do not deserve unkindness. You do not deserve to be treated like trash. You do not deserve just the scraps of living.

Please listen: Life has been unkind to you. It's okay to admit that. It doesn't mean that you are a victim or a weakling.

Perhaps, at times, I have been a part of that unkindness. I'm sorry for the whole fucking system and my part in it.

I am sorry.

I am sorry.

And the tears I shed right now aren't a facade. It's just that they don't mean enough. For you. For me. For anyone. I am sorry.

May you experience the better God has for you.

Here,
take this gift,
I was reserving it for some hero,
speaker, or general,
One who should serve the good old cause,
the great idea, the progress and
freedom of the race,
Some brave confronter of despots,
some daring rebel;
But I see that what I was reserving belongs to you
just as much as to any.

WALT WHITMAN
From
'Leaves of Grass'
('To a Certain Cantatrice')

Introduction
by Mimi German

In the winter of 2023, I met with Oregon Poet Laureate, Kim Stafford, at a coffee shop in Northwest Portland to discuss poetry and my work with unhoused communities in the city. My first book of poetry[1] was written during my years as a volunteer outreach worker and advocate for my friends struggling on the street. Kim suggested that I consider creating a poetry book to bring support and kindness to these communities, poems that could provide momentary uplift and perhaps even joy.

It took me weeks of consideration before moving forward with this project. The main question I had in my head was, how can we bring uplifting words to people who are in a 24/7 fight for survival from one day to the next and make those poems real. It struck me finally, that if anything could bring a bit of compassion and love to someone, it could be done through poetry.

I began to focus on how this book, like my first, could create a unification of love and compassion, rather than outrage and divisiveness, through poetry written by poets both housed and unhoused, in America and across the world, expressly for people living on the streets.

---

[1] *The Gravel Weight of Stars* (The Poetry Box, Portland, Oregon, 2022)

I reached out to my dear friend, *Karlostheunhappy* in the United Kingdom, to help me create this book, making selections from the great father of American poetry, Walt Whitman. These poems are shown in *italics* and are marked 'WW'. They come from a range of works, including his most famous, *Leaves of Grass*.

With the help and support of *Street Roots* newspaper in Portland, this book has become a reality. Our hope is that you will purchase these books and give them to people whom you meet on the street, struggling with the day-to-day nightmare of being unhoused. In this way, you will help spread love instead of hate, compassion instead of indifference, to make this world a bit better than it was yesterday.

Gratefully,

Mimi German
Oregon Beat Poet Laureate 2023-2025

TABLE OF CONTENTS

She Said

by Mimi German

the rain is sweet today
soft with the taste of spring
the patter against my tent roof
lulls me back to sleep

To those who've fail'd,
in aspiration vast…
…I'd rear a laurel-cover'd monument,
High, high above the rest —
To all cut off before their time,
Possess'd by some strange spirit of fire,
Quench'd by an early death.

WW
from
'Sands at Seventy'

Mimi German & Karlostheunhappy

No One Works
as Hard as the Homeless
by Fred Voss

For every ear-shattering WHAP of Frank's big hammer
smashing steel block down in vice
his wife Jane slides
a $5 bill into the palm of a homeless man or lady
in shadow of alley for every day
Frank spends wrestling
sharp-edged slabs of aluminum
and heaving 3-jawed 100-pound tools steel chucks
Jane slips
a $5 bill into the hand of a man from Mexico playing
mariachi
on a purple squeeze box
on a downtown Long Beach Street corner or a woman
with nothing but a blanket and her outstretched palm
on a dirty sidewalk
no one works as hard as the homeless
hiking up and down alleys all day and night
searching our trash dumpsters
pulling out bottles and tin cans
pushing them into giant plastic bags they fill and hoist
over their shoulders and haul over bridges
toward recycling centre dimes
so they can get a loaf of bread
as CEOs

sit in offices bigger than luxury apartments
daydreaming
about their golf games or their next vacation in Biarritz
no one works as hard as the homeless
somehow remembering how to smile
walking hundreds of miles a week combing our alleys
for scraps of food
somehow going on
living on raw will and air and a chess game
or a bottle of cheap vodka shared
in a park or under a freeway overpass
and Jane pays them
for every chip of red-hot steel
flying off razor-sharp cutter to land on Frank's neck
smoking
Jane is sliding a $5 bill into the palm of a man or
woman
on the edge of giving up hope
and dying
because no one works as hard as the homeless
taking the next step
when no one cares
no one works as hard as the homeless
never stopping
barely sleeping
hardly knowing where to turn next
as they hold onto each $5 bill Janes gives them
like it was all that was left
of human kindness.

Mimi German & Karlostheunhappy

It Hurts So Good To Be Alive

by Bill Lewis

Don't take this
Pain away.

It's mine not yours.
I have a right to it.

It is like the outline
Of a body that can

No longer be touched,

A missing smile that

Nobody ever
    bothered to photograph.

So hands off, I own it.

Don't take this
Pain away

Don't give me
Morphine or *ganja*,

Mood elevators or
Mood depressors,

Red wine or religion,
Revolution or whisky,

Tobacco or therapy
Flowers or
Feel-good movies,

This is my pain.
I own it.

It hurts so good.

It hurts so good
To be.

It hurts so good
To be alive.

Mimi German & Karlostheunhappy

Bread

by George Wallace

To those with whom we wait,
not singing like the bards,
not chasing the fox, not
waxing poetic and idle
like lords with plenty of
wick to burn, but in plain
light of day, beneath the
stone parapet, or dreaming
at the fountain, thru which the
bird of immortality has flown;
not gathering by the river,
not standing with the people
in the burning plaza, shouting
for the overthrow of some
sad government, but silent
as love itself, breaking bread;
we entreaty those who have
moved or tortured us, we drink
with those who we have somehow
made temporarily whole, we
speak calmly to anyone who
has fought in a war they could not
understand, and who cannot
lay their weapon down; and
we dance with the lonely people
at the bar, with hearts not yet

broken, with the confused
and untutored, we dance!
For the mystery of resurrection
to rise like music in mountains,
for the sun to break over ruined
river valleys that commerce has
scarred, but could not hold;
and we travel alone and we travel
together, with headlights stolen from the law;

and we seek peace, peace! By the river,
in the valley, in the tenement, peace
to the homeless and the unsheltered,
peace to the hypocrite and the unloved;
peace to the shop girl in the tartan dress,
waiting at the rainy bus shelter
with her parcel of bread

Mimi German & Karlostheunhappy

Stranger,
If you passing meet me
and desire to speak to me,
why should you not speak to me?
And why should I not speak to you?

WW
from
'Leaves of Grass'
('To You')

Flowers of the Litter

Stoned

by Karlostheunhappy

To all those
who have lost childhood littered in the past
lost friends broken in the mess
lost homes with absolutely no desire to curl into
winter's cold palm,
who settle for bread, denied even a dream of roses
who have tasted the grip of ecstasy & cough up its
anchoring hold.
To all those
who cherish the sun
I say, you deserve more than some crummy
            overworked, underfunded civic office.
You deserve humanity
of which your unholy circumstance
reveals is in terrible famine.

For you, then, there is only yourself
and the everyday saints.
Together we offer these few poems
as blankets of hope.
Useless as they are,
they are at least a stone into which your existence has
            been scratched
before being kicked along the road.

Mimi German & Karlostheunhappy

Have you ever seen a stone stand up?
I dream it happens.
I hope.
We wish.
And, friend, you will.

Flowers of the Litter

Was somebody asking to see the soul?
See, your own shape and countenance, persons,
substances, beasts, the trees,
The running rivers,
the rocks and sands.

All hold spiritual joys
and afterwards loosen them;
How can the real body ever die
and be buried?

Of your real body
and any man's or woman's real body,
Item for item
it will elude the hands of the corpse-cleaners

and pass to fitting spheres,
Carrying what has accrued to it
from the moment of birth to the moment of death. WW
from
'Starting from Paumanok'
(beginning of verse #13)

Mimi German & Karlostheunhappy

Haiku

by Resa Alboher

The tall cactuses
rest against the vast blue sky…
When will we rest too?

"We will get through this…"
my mother tells me in dreams.
Irises open…

Ducks visit the pond
before flying south…
We want to fly too…

This is the meal equally set,
this the meat for natural hunger,
It is for the wicked just the same
as the righteous,
I make appointments with all,
I will not have a single person slighted
or left astray…

This hour I tell things in confidence,
I might not tell everyone,
but I will tell you.

WW
from
'Song of Myself'
(excerpts of verse #19)

Mimi German & Karlostheunhappy

Can You Hear This?

by Lynnette Snook

Through the holy spirit in me

I tell you

The world has been created for us

How do we partake in it

Some choose to be good

Some choose to be thieves

But ask a thief if he can rub two nickels together any

day of the week

The reality is we don't take this with us

The hearse doesn't carry a hitch

So, love within

Let it spew unto others

Remember God takes care of even the sparrow

Take a look at yourself deep inside
Give the best of what you have
Feed someone else who's hungry
That's the joy
Having the love and the time
The willingness to understand this
It takes a day to live a day

Mimi German & Karlostheunhappy

I saw in Louisiana a live-oak growing,
All alone stood it and the
moss hung down from the branches,
Without any companion it grew
there uttering joyous leaves of dark green,
And its look, rude, unbending, lusty,
made me think of myself…

WW
from
'Calamus'
(opening lines of
'I Saw In Louisiana a Live-Oak Growing…')

Flowers of the Litter

In a Snow Storm

by Pankhuri Sinha

Out and about, in a 7 feet
Snow dumping snow storm
Beside the frozen glass wall
Of the bus stop
A human figure, huddled
Is it a blanket or just a larger overcoat?
A hand shaking in temperatures below zero
The light of a cigarette
Twinkling like fire dance
On white ice! Flame colour
Engulfs all! Yet winter lingers, questions burn!
Who was supposed to come and get you and
Who couldn't come? How
Did you, when did you
Walk out of your life?
Did no one follow you?
Person or state?
Don't you have a social
Security number?
You see, I am waiting
For mine, since the past
Fourteen years or longer
I lost count, you see, I am

An immigrant that got too
Close! But how did you get
Pushed away?
How did
They lose you?
Can't you find your way
Back, my friend?
I am trying too!

Flowers of the Litter

Neither a servant
nor a master I,
I take no sooner a large price
than a small price,
I will have my own whoever enjoys me,
I will be even with you
and you shall be even with me.

WW
from
'A Song for Occupations'

Mimi German & Karlostheunhappy

A Single Step

by Kat Black

Accept the obstacles you face
In this moment, it may turn out to
Be your greatest gift.

There's something to be said for
The compassion the gray streets
Have to offer.
In just one day so much can happen,
In just one day your whole
Life may change.
Even a journey of 1000 miles starts
With a single step.

Some days it seems like they're only steps
Backwards, but the gratitude you have
By what is received outweighs what
Has been given.
The truth lies in your heart
I have no ego in this, the smallest
Change can lead to the biggest
Reward.
Take that step, find your path
The street is your opportunity to this
Life you are living. We only have one
Life to live and it is our own.

It takes courage to say that you don't
Know, it takes bravery to make a
Path on your own. I wish you luck,
I wish you love, it only takes
That first step to see where you'll go.
The essence of life is to communicate love.

Mimi German & Karlostheunhappy

All the hapless silent lovers,
All the prisoners in the prisons,
all the righteous and the wicked,
All the joyous, all the sorrowing,
all the living, all the dying,
Pioneers! O Pioneers!

. . .

These are of us,
they are with us...

WW
from
'Birds of Passage'

Flowers of the Litter

Cannot Sweep Nature

by Bronwyn Carver

On path
of freshly turned dirt
from the last sweep that came through mounds of
debris and whatnots
hide within trip-traps
Of muddy earth
Yet even though souls
From this place
have been scattered
North south east west
Upside down
One lone daffodil appeared
pushed up through the mud
that is the soil
Bright golden yellow with its almost
Orange trumpet center
proclaiming a hearkening
hearkening for Hope to take shape
Love to blossom once more

I will confront

these shows of the day and night,

I will know if I am to be less than they,

I will see if I am not as majestic as they,

I will see if I am not as subtle and real as they,

I will see if I am able to be less generous than they,

I will see

if I have no meaning...

WW
from
'By Blue Ontario's Shore'

Flowers of the Litter

Dedication of Thanks

by Joseph "Whitecloud" Smits

I remember when I reach
Out to you. You listened
We talk for awhile
Lost contact over the years
But I still follow you
Listen to your music
Just wanted to tell you thank you
You and so many people have
Saved my life.
I know I have done the same
And will continue to do so
But I can't take credit
I give it to God,
People who never gave up on me.

Mimi German & Karlostheunhappy

Courage yet, my brother or my sister!
Keep on —
Liberty is to be subserv'd whatever occurs;
That is nothing that is quell'd by one or two failures,
or any number of failures,
Or by the indifference or ingratitude of the people,
or by any unfaithfulness,
Or the show of the tushes of power,
soldiers, cannon, penal statutes.

What we believe in
waits latent forever…

WW
from
'Autumn Rivulets'
(opening of
'To A Foil'd European Revolutionaire')

Flowers of the Litter

Feels Like Home

by Dumpsta D

Always carry yourself with dignity
            And grace.
            Never wipe the tears from your face.
                Like a badge of honor they have
Earned their place.

No one else has walked a mile in your
            Blues, what you have bravely
                Endured they would never choose.

You were only given this one amazing
            Chance. Your one beautiful
            Life. Your invitation to the
                Dance.

                All you desire and
      Deserve   lies just on the other
Side of fear.   To live in this
      Spectacular
now is the reason you're here.

            Never quit, never submit.
            Never die quietly inside.
            Wave like a flag of resistance
            Your humanity and pride!

Mimi German & Karlostheunhappy

You are dearly loved,
　　　You never walk alone.

In the comfort of your
　　　　　Own skin,
　　　You will always
　　　Have a place
　　　To call

　　　Home.

Flowers of the Litter

Not till the sun excludes you
do I exclude you,
Not till the waters refuse to glisten for you
and the leaves to rustle for you,
do my words
refuse to glisten and rustle for you.

WW
from
'Autumn Rivulets'
(excerpt from
'To A Common Prostitute')

Mimi German & Karlostheunhappy

Improvising

by Daniel Toole

Street Roots is closed and I'm out of papers
I grab a stack of Willamette Weeklies
Nobody will notice

Why, who makes much of miracles?

As to me
I know of nothing else but miracles,
Whether I walk the streets of Manhattan,
Or dart my sight over the roofs of houses
toward the sky,
Or wade with naked feet along the beach
just in the edge of the water
Or stand under trees in the woods…

Or sit at table at dinner with the rest

WW
from
'Autumn Rivulets'
(excerpt from 'Miracles')

Mimi German & Karlostheunhappy

Flowers of the Litter

by Mimi German & Karlostheunhappy

take all flowers off the street
wash them away
that is the way
the state would have it

i collect petals
like others do cans
place them in eternity
in the pages of my heart

remember when
hope
was something you could remember?
when you weren't full with emptiness & fault?

love exists in the essence
of breath, in mountain rain
in the harsh of winter's pain
in the bite of raw

home too long in the ignore
relief yr only not friend –
crowds stride thru urban fields
litter-lined, bulging belonging carts & wrinkles

what use poets?

i give you these flowers
while i mantra your name

i give you these flowers
while i mantra your name

Mimi German & Karlostheunhappy

Wild(er)ness

by Mimi German

the say nothing
is out here   that there
is the middle

          of nowhere

but here
exactly   here
you find your   where
on earth
your   who   you are   your   you

you are whole   here
where time is the existence of a sun
and a lizard who tells you that living is just luck

KOSMOS

...

Who, constructing the house
of himself or herself,
not for a day
but for all time
sees races, eras, dates, generations,
The past, the future,
dwelling there,
like space,
inseparable
together.

WW
from
'Autumn Rivulets'
(excerpt from 'Kosmos')

Mimi German & Karlostheunhappy

Prayer of the Homeless

by Maddy Brown-Clark

The city lights
Were like stars in an urban sky
And I knelt on my knees to pray
Please God protect me from the streets
And urban decay
To face life another day
Most of my friends
Will beg steal or lie
To get their next meal
Do or die
Or spend afternoons
Standing in line
For some satisfaction to feel
But there is a light
At the end of the day
With every prayer I say
Sing Angels sing
Show this nomad the way
And fly me to a home on your wings.

Maddy Brown-Clark

passed away in October of 2023
before the publication of this book was completed

Others may praise what they like;
But I, from the banks of the running Missouri,
praise nothing in art or aught else,
Till it has well inhaled the atmosphere of this river,
also the western prairie-scent,
And exudes it all again.

WW
from
'Autumn Rivulets'
('Others May Praise What They Like' (in its righteous
entirety!))

Flowers of the Litter

Remembrance

by George McCarthy

.........so squeezed together.....so
pressed into place.... wrenched up
and folded over bone ratcheted
against bone until memories,
feelings, thoughts burst in
overlap....juice locked in a bag...
symphony drawn down to one
small string...to soft breathing in
darkness....like sea stars torn apart
by crabs, chewed by sharks,
rendered to bits of crimson....
patches of zebra skin..... ribbons
of electric blue----so much
devoured and destroyed but the
whispers of memory......like a song
of remembrance that keeps whole
what's been taken away--- that
spreads who you are around you
so you can reach out and grow
back into yourself.....stretch your
limbs, and touch your
fingertips........

Mimi German & Karlostheunhappy

I do not think seventy years
is the time of a man or woman.
Nor that seventy millions of years
is the time of a man or woman,
Nor that years will ever stop the existence of me,
or any one else.

WW
from
'Autumn Rivulets'
(excerpt from
'Who Learns My Lesson Complete?')

Flowers of the Litter

Sunshine

by Joseph "Whitecloud" Smits

I love when the sun comes up
Seeing the sunrise and sunsets
Are breathtaking and lift my
Spirits, without the sunshine
Feel cold and incomplete

The beautiful colors in the
Sun are amazing and beautiful
When the rain comes in it
Makes my body feel pain
But the rainbow beaming
With shining rays from the
Sun consumes me with joy

Mimi German & Karlostheunhappy

Ever the undiscouraged, resolute, struggling
soul of man…

…Ever the soul dissatisfied,
curious, unconvinced at last;
Struggling to-day the same—battling the same.

WW
from
the poem
'Life'
from
'Sands at Seventy'

Flowers of the Litter

The Chronicles of My Life

by Arc Angel Mykaiel

Part 1
Life seems 2 be
Turned upside down
Please don't take my
Smile. No longer feel
As if I'm on solid
Ground.
Light is winning
& ego still tries
To tell me so many
Lies. I have broken
Old ties & cut the
Cords.
Anxiety is so high
Vibrating so much
Please mother/father
I give you my will
& my trust.

Mimi German & Karlostheunhappy

Part 2
Crying out to God

Why so much
Suffering & pain

Why was 2 births
If but, to feel
Pain, Father, Mother

God why don't you
Let my life be in
Vain.

Just when I
Could not hold on
Any longer

She divulged
Herself to me which
Has made me much
Stronger.

Knowing she doesn't
Make mistakes
2 still having so
Much trouble of
Letting go of what
No longer serves
Me

Flowers of the Litter

Being shown so
Much love & beauty

Please Mother / Father
God do not let
Me fail.

Knowing I've
Been awakened know
Please do not let
Me fail.

Mimi German & Karlostheunhappy

This and When

by Bronwyn Carver

This is the time of year
When birds sing their songs
At 5:30 am in the morn
Til night comes to tuck them in

When the rain changes its mind
Decides to slumber
Several months of silence
Till it remembers *Casablanca*
And cries

This is the time of year
I think of outdoor patio bars
Of San Francisco and Portland
Where sun gathers with people

When noble is the sunshine
And all the kool kids drink
Koolade now made for grownups
Wearing sunshades over reddened eyes
Talking passionately of nothings

This is the time of year
You and I venture out and about
Jackets no longer required
As the universe leads the way

Flowers of the Litter

When we go with the flow
And laugh out loud at private jokes
Whilst you suggest we visit hell
I hold your hand
And together we fall

This is the time of year
For rememberness
Yet how do I remember
When I haven't forgot you

Mimi German & Karlostheunhappy

I walk by myself —
I stand and look at the stars,
which I think now
I never realized before.

Now I absorb
immortality and peace...

WW
from
'Whispers…'
(excerpts from 'Night on the Prairies')

Flowers of the Litter

Whispers in the Wind

by Joseph "Whitecloud" Smits

1. Sometimes people might not
   think the wind talks.

2. It really does and when
   the wind is upset

3. It roars like a lion
   but when the wind is calm it's like

4. A baby cuddled in the
   arms of their mother or father.

5. The wind definitely speaks to me in volumes
   sometimes depending on my mood

6. Sometimes just what I see when I feel
   the sweet touch reminds me of the Angels
   who are now in heaven.

7. Whispers of the wind
   I'm alive, I'm alive.

Mimi German & Karlostheunhappy

The homeward bound
and the outward bound,
The beautiful lost swimmer...

...

I swear they are all beautiful,
Every one that sleeps
is beautiful,
every thing in the dim light
is beautiful...

The soul is
always
beautiful...

WW
from
'The Sleeper'
(excerpts from #7)

Flowers of the Litter

Why have you forsaken me

by Daniel Toole

My God, My God
Oh my God
You never forsook me

Mimi German & Karlostheunhappy

The Color of Hope

by Karlostheunhappy

give up the night
as easy I gave up the fight
when council contractors came,
removed my voice
removed all cries
removed fresh cities
told us to move on
to some other dying nowhere

and then
just when I was all out of hope…

Minimalist poem

by Karlostheunhappy

waking

cold

early

sun

breaks
the cloud

Mimi German & Karlostheunhappy

I announce justice triumphant,
I announce uncompromising
liberty and equality,

...

I announce a life that shall be copious,
vehement, spiritual, bold
Salute me — salute the days once more.
Peal the old cry once more.

...

Camerado, this is no book,
Who touches this touches a man...
It is I you hold
and who holds you,
I spring from the pages into your arms

...

WW
from
'Songs of Parting'
(excerpts from 'So Long!')

Flowers of the Litter

Choices

by Kat Black

It blows my mind when I don't think
That much can surprise me but something
Happens and gets my blood rising.

How do you know that I'm not hungry too,
And as I walked inside to wash my
Hands you stole my sandwich and my drink too.

How little do you know how much wind my
Threadbare coat lets in, so as I stand
With a thermal cup of tea was the only
Thing to keep me from freezing.

As we slept on tiny mats with
Gossamer blankets you could pick
To cover your head, wrap your
Arms or take off those wet shoes
And warm up your toes.

Carefully choose for what gets left out certainly
Will disappear I understand that the
Struggle is real but we're in this
Together trying to heal but really
The only thing you can think of to
Do is steal from the ones that don't

Mimi German & Karlostheunhappy

Have anything either gluttony and
Sloth is such a gross human order
And you're going so low to get your
Thrills from the person next to you
Fighting to just continue.

Where's your price, when's it finally
Enough. We all have a choice on
How to survive this life.
We're all looking for a simple
Truth to live by.
We all get the same option,
We all feel the evil eye stare,
It's all left in the hands of fate.
Each man, woman, and child is left
With a very simple thing, the "choice"
To decide who they are, who they want
To be.

To choose between what's wrong and right.

This world is filled with so many battles
That no one should ever fight.
We can't do all the good in the
World but the world needs all the
Good we can do.

Flowers of the Litter

So take your time it's what we got
If trust is the question then love is
The answer to just keep living.

I don't know who's right about the
Beginning or how full the middle
Should be but someday will be the
Ending. This road we travel this
Journey of the unknown take in the
Trip, do all you can with your time.

The final destination is just that
A vast emptiness where we have
No more time, and our lives
Our choices whatever they may be
No one is going to want something
And let it slip away, that's not how
Our hearts work, we "choose" to
Love this way!

Mimi German & Karlostheunhappy

Five Poems

by Shaggy

Autism Awareness April

Autism Awareness April
Suess set
Poems
blu**E** peace
Red peace
sha**G**gy
to peac**E**
th**R**ee peace
Street roots

from 'Red Peace'

Promised life, I get the gist
It's served with side of bitterness

from 'Blue Peace'

Another week of feeling weak
A warm, dry seat is what I seek

Flowers of the Litter

from 'To Peace'
Seeds to fall in our heart's cracks
> Assist us to achieve our max
> To help avoid being conceited
> Lest we're the ones that's being cheated
On the right, we start to blame
> Soon after add a heap of shame
Take a step outside the frame
> All that's left shows we're the same
The odds are stacked, I'm betting we
> Won't live to see our legacy
> If anything our destiny
> Should be to set each other free

from 'Three Peace'
Although it's hard to see the virtue
In letting go of that which haunts you
An endless guest to seal a win
Cause those who lose
Choose to desert you

Mimi German & Karlostheunhappy

Only the Broken

by Eagle Spits

Only the broken can write poetry
only the broken let in light
only the broken really see the stars in the night
We worship a homeless man on Sunday's then ignore
                          him all week
We say we give a voice to the voiceless then don't listen
                          when they speak
We quibble about doctrine without love in our hearts
Justice is love in action but does it ever start
Only the broken can heal us
only the broken can feel
only the broken can be open to what is real
We teach the poor our doctrine which runs as shallow
                          as our masks
we say they should be grateful yet ignore them when
                          they ask
where is our tomorrow in this systems schemes
We talk about salvation then we crush their dreams
Wake up you sleepy children
open your hearts and minds
the broken are our siblings
the naked lead the blind

After the dazzle of day is gone,
Only the dark, dark night shows to my eyes
the stars;

WW
from
'Sands at Seventy'

Mimi German & Karlostheunhappy

To Take Shape

by Bronwyn Carver

I am looking skyward
my back flat on ground
of inken soil
looking through squinted eyes
as sun of lemon yellow
kisses lids bathes my face
In blazing light
looking I am at clouds
of cotton white taking shape
looking for you
but wind blows those outlines to outliers and I
I am left still searching scanning
for even a memory to take shape
In my mind's eye
I see you
Standing casual laughing at
Someone's jokes I think
You turn and those blue eyes
I miss that smile
Those eyes
And I smile and laugh
At the joke unheard
Cause it seemed like
The right thing to do
And so to see you
Longer
As I long for us

Old Friend

by Mimi German

beneath the tree
of rooted loss

you sleep in love
inside the shatter

remember the bird
who chose you for its mission
to invest in living

she flew to you
with infinite love
to make you shimmer
in the golden light of days

you are seventy-one rings strong
weathered but able
to dance upon the rising sun

Mimi German & Karlostheunhappy

Language, be it remember'd,
is not an abstract construction of the learn'd,
or of dictionary-makers,
but is something arising
out of the work, needs, ties, joys, affections, tastes,
of long generations of humanity,
and has its bases
broad and low,
close to
the ground.

WW
from
'Slang in America'

Flowers of the Litter

*Failing to fetch me at first
keep encouraged,
Missing me one place
search another,
I stop somewhere
waiting for you.*

WW
from
'Song of Myself'
(last lines)

Mimi German & Karlostheunhappy

AFTERWORD

I am very grateful for the opportunity to work on this project. I know of none other more qualified, more gifted, to reflect the reality of the houseless streets and to do so as poetically than Mimi German.

Generally, poems are a poor bulwark against poverty, injustice and strife. But they can be a flag of a kind.

We've tried to include work that inspires and reflects - not shout ideals. But no one can deny the absurdity of a world where only the few enjoy riches.

Although it has the capability, it seems humanity, ironically, lacks the humanity to resolve these issues. This collection does not attempt to solve this crisis. At most all it can do is - hopefully - provide a moment's consolation, a moment's recognition of the struggle itself.

We have chosen to pepper the text with the words of the grandfather of American poetry, Walt Whitman. In doing so we hope to show humanity at pinnacle, all kindness and potential fulfilled.

Mimi was clear from the outset: this is a book of poetry for people who generally don't read poetry, selected primarily *for* those struggling on the streets. It should rise from those very streets, whilst at the same time drop

Flowers of the Litter

stanzas like a loving kind of rain. It seeks not to exclude in any way, and hopes education or opportunity precludes none.

It is with love that I hope we achieved that.

Karlostheunhappy
gloomyforpleasure.com

About the Authors

Mimi German is an American poet, subversive artist, advocate for the unhoused, and queer childless cat lady dividing her time between life in the wilderness of Oregon's Steens Mountain where she lives with her partner. and the urban strife of Portland, OR. She has written four books of poetry since 2022, culminating with Flowers of the Litter, co-edited by Mimi German and Carl Spiby from the UK, a collection of poems written by both unhoused and housed poets across the world.

Mimi German has worked extensively with unhoused communities in Portland and worked as an advocate inside Portland's city hall where she often used her poetry as testimony against arbitrary rules against houselessness brought on by Mayor Ted Wheeler. Between 2015-2023, Mimi helped to establish unpermitted encampments run by houseless communities, much to the extreme ire and frustration of Portland's mayor, city council, cops, and park rangers. Her first book of poetry, Beneath the Gravel Weight of Stars released in 2022, wove her experiences and observations about the crisis of houselessness through her poetry. During the pandemic, Eye Publish Ewe published Mimi's third book, Where Grasses Bend as well as WAR POEMS Israel- Gaza/The First 100 Days of Carnage which has also become an art installation.

German's poetry has been published in numerous journals and books including New Generation Beats Anthologies, in Maintenant 18/ Journal of Contemporary Dada Writing and Art, in the Clarion Quarterly Journal #2, in Walt Whitman's Corner in the Long Islander, and in the UK in International Times(IT) and Steel JackDaw Magazine. She was named Oregon's first New Beat Generation Poet Laureate (2023-2025) by the National Beat Poetry Foundation.

Fred Voss lives in Long Beach, California and is the author of numerous collections of poetry from 1991's 'Goodstone' to 'Someday, There Will Be Machine Shops Full of Roses' (2023) and the novel 'Making America Strong' (2015). He abandoned a PhD in English lit at University of California to go work in a machine shop, and that 50 years became the inspiration for 'Someday..'.Smokestack Books said of this last collection establish Voss as the heir to Charles Bukowski, Philip Levine and Robert Tressell.

George Wallace (b 1949) is writer in residence at the Walt Whitman Birthplace in New York, author of 41 chapbooks, and a fixture of the NYC poetry performance scene. A poet and recording artist, he is adjunct professor of English at Pace University in Manhattan. George travels internationally to share his work, has been invited to major festivals in the US, UK, Europe and South America (Ledbury UK, Medellin Colombia, Woody Guthrie Festival Oklahoma), and has received numerous international honors and awards, including Festival Laureate, Ditet e Naimit, Tetova North Macedonia; Orpheus Prize, Plovdiv Bulgaria; Alexander Prize, Unesco-Piraeus, Salamis Greece; Aristotle Prize, International Poetry Festival, Naoussa Greece; Centro Studii Archivio d'Occidente Award, Lavis Italy; Naji Naaman Literary Award, Beirut Lebanon; and Poet of the Year, Boao China.

Bill Lewis, from England, was one of the legendary Medway Poets Group along with Billy Childish, Sexton Ming, Charles Thomson and Rob Earl. He has performed his poems in Europe, Latin America and North America and has been published in magazines, journals and anthologies all over the world. Some of his poems have been translated into French, Spanish, Italian and his short stories into German.

In addition, Lewis has been broadcast on television and radio on both sides of the Atlantic and has carried out readings, workshops and lectures at Literary Festivals (including the International Cambridge Poetry Festival), hospitals, prisons, schools and universities and he was the first Writer-in-Residence at the Brighton Festival (1985).

Lewis was one of the original 13 founder members of the Stuckist Movement. He has since gone on to disseminate the ideas and theories that have emerged from Remodernism. He also appeared in Michael Horovitz's anthology, the 'Grandchildren of Albion'. Bill's books include 'Sparrowhawk & other poems' (2022), 'In The House Of Ladders' (2012) and 'The Long Ago And Eternal Now' (2017). He continues to write and paint, with many of his publications featuring his own art.

Karlostheunhappy is the author of the Gloomy for Pleasure poetry collection 'OBLIVION: 200 Seasons of Pain & Magic' and the soon to be release sequel 'FLUX: the turning leaves'. His work has featured in the leading Beat magazine, Beatdom, and numerous anthologies including 2024's 'After Hours' a Beat anthology by the Broken Spine Press and IT (International Times). He also he read at Oxford's Blackwells for Kerouac's centenary.

He was secretary of the Forest of Dean Stop the War campaign in 2003 and a lifelong CND member. He runs an employee-owned software business where the engines of their success are the benefactors of that success. He was named Beat Poet Laureate (England) for 2022-23 by the Beat Poetry Foundation and was editor at BeatSurreal a 90s underground litzine, and co-editor for the Forest of Dean & Wye Valley Clarion, a local socialist monthly. An annual of Beatsurreal is due in 2024 through the Gloomy for Pleasure press. Born in Newport, Wales, he has lived all his life in the Forest of Dean, Gloucestershire.

Resa Alboher is one of the founding editors of St Petersburg Review, on the editorial board of Springhouse Journal, edits fiction for Running Wild Press/Rize, and has been a lecturer in the Summer Literary Seminars International programs. She writes across genre and her work has appeared in publications including River Dog Zine, Cold Moon Journal, Roads & Kingdoms, Cosmonauts Avenue, Trash Panda, Scapegoat Review, Black Heart Magazine, Rewire Me, Mango Salute, Have a NYC 2: New York Short Stories, Maintenant 5, Rattle, and Radar Productions. She feels in her heart and in her bones that poetry can heal this world.

The Street Poets featured in this book

All of the street poets in this book live in and around Portland, Oregon. Many are vendors, writers, and journalists for the Street Roots Newspaper and come to Street Roots for poetry classes weekly. These poets are members of our community. All are survivors. And some are no longer with us. It is an honor to have their work and creative expression in this book.

Lynette Snook
Kat Black
Bronwyn Carver
Joseph "Whitecloud" Smits
Dumpsta D
Daniel Toole
Maddy Brown-Clark
George McCarthy
Arc Angel Mykaiel
Shaggy

Pankhuri Sinha is a bilingual young poet and story writer from India, who has lived in North America for 14 years and has two books of poems published in English, three collections of stories published in Hindi, eight collections of poetries published in Hindi, with many more lined up. Has won many prestigious, national-international awards, and has been translated in over twenty-seven languages. Her writing is dominated by themes of exile and immigration, gender equality and environmental concerns.

Eagle Spits is a punk poet and founder of Punk 4 The Homeless who lives in Nottingham, England. He is a writer and homeless advocate of the punkest kind.

About EYEPUBLISHEWE

Eye publish ewe is a brand new publishing company, founded in San Francisco. Art, music, video, poetry, and other literature will find inclusive shelter here. Quality work produced by the artists' hearts, minds, and souls rather than commercial interests will have this as a home. All are welcomed with open minds and hearts and eyes to the future. Together we will publish art for humanity's sake.

EPE titles

Where Grasses Bend: Poems from Portland to Steens Mountain in the Time of Plagues by **Mimi German** ISBN: 979-8-9870259-5-6

WAR POEMS : Israel-Gaza/The First 100 Days of Carnage by **Mimi German** ISBN:979-8-9898764-4-0

The Green Notebook: Poems on Family, Relationships, Spirituality, Self-Enquiry, Recovery, ACA, Disruption, Death, Walking Through the Mirror, and Cats by **John Angell Grant** ISBN: 979-8-9870259-6-3

Morning Tanka : A journal of thank you notes between lovers, California poems in the style of traditional Japanese form poetry translated by Yuri Miki by **Dane Ince** and **Mercedes Dugger** ISBN: 979-8-9898764-0-2

Crimson Stain: Poems Inspired by King's Letter from Jail, Real Life, and A Facet of Blood Diamond Culture by **Dee Allen**. ISBN: 979-8-9898764-3-3

Destiny Murder!: A Poetic Odyssey of Pulp Poems in the Beat Noir Style Concerning the Dutch Angle of Strange Dreams, Erotic, Ambivalent, Cruel and Cynical by **Dane Ince** ISBN: 979-8-9870259-8-7

EPE Titles Coming Soon

A House without Walls: Existential Journeys and Love Poems to Mexico by **Lesley Constable**

La Naturaleza del Amor: Poems in Spanish and English by **Martin Del Toro Gutierrez**

www.ingramcontent.com/pod-product-compliance
Lightning Source LLC
Chambersburg PA
CBHW020327130626
46549CB00003B/1048